Stories

of Grace:

CHANGED HEARTS

CHANGED LIVES

Burke Women's Ministry

Dedication

This book is dedicated to you, the reader.

TABLE OF CONTENTS

Go Tell Your Story

Inspired by a sermon from BCC Missions Pastor,
Alec Zacaroli

Go tell your story
Go tell the world
What Christ has done for you

Go tell your story
Go tell the world
How He has changed you

Go tell the story
Don't hide it away
There's someone who needs to hear

Go tell the story
Don't hide it away
How He can change them too

Go tell your story
Tell of His hope
Salvation for everyone who believes

Go tell your story
Tell of His hope
Salvation for everyone who calls on His name

Go tell His story
And how He saves
Shout it from the mountain tops

Go tell His story
And how He saves
Shout it in the valley

So, what is your story
And who will you tell
There is a world that needs to hear

So, what is your story
And what is your story
And when will you share it
  —S. Bowman

Heart Knowledge Beyond Doubt

We often hear the phrases "head knowledge" and "heart knowledge" in reference to the ways we can know someone. "Head knowledge" is the facts about a person, whereas "heart knowledge" is our personal experience with that person. For instance, I know that George Washington was the first president of the United States, that he served two terms, and that before the Revolutionary War, he fought on the side of the British during the French and Indian War. But I have no personal experience of the man because he lived 200 years ago. So, my knowing George Washington is all "head knowledge" but not "heart knowledge."

When it comes to knowing God, the same kinds of knowledge apply. I can rattle off a list of God's characteristics, such as He is holy, righteous, omnipotent, omniscient, and omnipresent, loving, patient, kind and forgiving. But this is a list of things I learned about Him by rote. On the other hand, I know God personally when I experience Him firsthand, and there is nothing that could convince me otherwise.

Many biblical characters had this kind of "heart knowledge". Moses knew without a doubt that God is holy from his experience at the burning bush when God commanded him to take off his sandals because he was on holy ground. Moses was in awe of the mystifying phenomenon in front of him. And Moses continued to show great reverence for God's holiness in his dealings with the pharaoh of Egypt. The 10 plagues that God sent to Egypt were all acts of judgment on a stubborn, pagan nation, as was the destruction of Egypt's army as they pursued the Israelites across the Red Sea. Moses' respect for God's holiness continued in his dealings with his own people, the

Israelites. In the wilderness when they disbelieved, God tested him time and time again. Moses would time and time again plead for mercy on the stubborn, stiff-necked people because of their lack of trust and belief in God. And it was a rash disregard for God's holy command to speak to but not strike the rock at Meribah that lost Moses the honor and privilege of leading the Israelites into the land promised them so long ago to their ancestors, Abraham, Isaac, and Jacob.

Peter, in the New Testament, knew in his heart that God was a forgiving God when Jesus charged him with the tremendous task of tending His fledgling flock of disciples, even after Peter had denied the Christ three times in one night just a few days earlier during Jesus' trumped-up nighttime trial.

And there have been times in my own life when I have had to ask myself, "What do I really believe about God beyond a shadow of a doubt?" One time came just after my husband and I were told by a neurologist at Children's Hospital in Washington, DC, that our six-month-old baby girl did indeed have cerebral palsy and that it was unknown whether or not she would be able to walk, talk, or even think normally. We were stunned and dismayed. People at our church tried to comfort us with the words, "It couldn't have happened to a better family" (to which I silently responded, "I can think of a better one—yours!"). I didn't know how to share my grief with my church family, but I knew I could share it with God. He was my safe place.

Not wanting my three young children to see my grief, I would hide in the bathroom and sob. Often, I would take a shower to drown out my crying as well as to wash away the tears. And from the very first day, the only scripture that came to mind was Jeremiah 29:11: "'I know the plans I have for you,' declares the Lord, 'plans for prosperity and not for disaster, to give you a future and a hope.'" I recited that verse over and over and over for Hannah, having no idea what the future held for her but trusting God to work this will for her. My only request was that He would protect her mind so that she could communicate with us. But I knew that was up to His will, too. This went on for nine months until one day I realized that I had not been in the bathroom pleading with God for several days. I suddenly realized that life could go on normally without any sorrow. It was going to be OK. By God's grace, we could do this, figure this out, take care of Hannah, and meet her needs for that day. God was in control; it would be all right.

And indeed, God has worked all things out for good and not for evil; He has and is giving her a future and hope. Although her body does not do what her brain would like it to do, she is a sharp young woman with goals in mind and a lot to offer. And she has hope that she will see Jesus one day and run and run to her heart's content in Heaven.

 Tina

Real and Personal Faith

Growing up in a small town in North Carolina, I was blessed to have been raised in a Christian home. My parents taught me about God and Jesus from an early age. They took my brothers and me to church regularly, led us as we prayed blessings over our meals and tucked us into bed each night with a Bible story. I believed in God and His greatness and had no reason to question His goodness nor His love for me.

By the time I was in high school, my mother had become involved in a Christian women's club, a ministry much like BCC's Breakaway and WOW. As she began to study the Bible with other women, she recognized her need for a *personal* relationship with Jesus. She came to understand that a life of faith is more than just checking the boxes of church attendance and doing certain religious practices. She recognized that Jesus wanted a relationship with her, that He wanted to be an integral part of her everyday thoughts and actions. She saw her need to release control of her life and to submit to His will and His ways. My dad admitted later that he was a bit concerned she might be "going off the deep end" in this new attitude towards faith, but secretly he began to read the Bible at his office each day. As he began diligently and consistently to read God's Word for himself, he, too, concluded that he needed Jesus as the Lord of his life.

My parents shared with me their excitement about this newfound relationship they had with Jesus, but I wasn't all that interested. I was a bit uncomfortable with their faith discussions, and honestly, I remained perfectly happy to continue "checking boxes." I soon headed off to college, but during my times home for holidays and summer breaks, I noticed a change in the atmosphere of our home. My parents' marriage had always been stable and our home a happy one, but I was observing our home gradually changing from a Christian home to a *Christ-centered* home. Although I didn't admit it to my parents at the time, I found myself attracted to this kind of real and personal faith that was evident in their lives.

Isn't it interesting how pride and obstinacy can prevent us from taking a step towards faith? For some reason, I was too proud and stubborn at that time to acknowledge my need for the same personal relationship with Jesus in my life. But God is good ... and He pursued me. After college I moved to Virginia Beach to teach school, and it was there that God finally softened my heart to Him through some long conversations with a friend. What this young man shared with me about Jesus was no different from what my parents had been sharing, but in God's perfect timing, my heart was ready to admit my need for Him. In a short time, I found a local church where God's Word was taught and where I could be in community with other believers.

Many years later, I still cherish God's Word, as it is primarily through His Word that He has revealed Himself to me. I have found His Word truly to be "a lamp to my feet and a light to my path" (Psalm 119:105) as I now live my life submitted to Him.

 Brenda

The Foundation of My Life

Before I surrendered to Christ, my identity was built on my family and my own abilities. Though I was raised in the church, I saw religion mostly as an obligation. On the outside I seemed to have it all, but on the inside, I struggled with lust, loneliness, and a desire to please others. I thought that I could solve my problems through my own works, only to realize that this was futile. When I was in high school, my parents divorced, and it felt like my identity was shattered. I fell into despair and was angry at God because I thought that He must have caused these things to happen.

When I went to college at Virginia Tech, I stumbled upon an event that was hosted by one of the Christian ministries on campus. At this event, I met the most authentic and kind students, who were sharing with me about their faith in God and asking deep questions about my life. I continued to go to events hosted by the ministry and even joined a small group. In this ministry, I met people who loved and served me in a genuine way. I witnessed people my age who were truly passionate about Jesus and lived out what they believed. At the weekly services, I continually heard about the good news of Jesus Christ. I began praying and reading my Bible on my own and came to understand how much God had been revealing His love for me through the actions of community and through His Word. During that time, God highlighted Psalm 34:18: "The Lord is near the brokenhearted and saves those who are crushed in spirit." By spring semester of freshman year, I had fully put my trust in Jesus Christ as my Lord and Savior. God showed me how much He cared for me by healing me of heartbrokenness, giving me a new identity, and showing me the power of forgiveness.

Since putting my trust in Jesus and walking in relationship with Him, I have been able to extend forgiveness to others because of the way God has forgiven and extended grace to me. I stopped pursuing my own selfish desires and began seeking God's righteousness and purposes for my life. Despair was replaced with joy. Through the help of the Holy Spirit, my relationships with my family began to mend. God also blessed me with amazing spiritual brothers and sisters in the body of Christ. I learned how to use my God-given gifts and talents to mentor and serve. After college, God called me to be a campus missionary, sharing the love of Christ with college students who were in a similar place as I was. My relationship with Christ is now the foundation of my life and how I operate in my church, community, family, and corporate job.

✿ Danielle

A Calm Exchange

Mine is not a unique testimony. In many ways, it's rather typical. I was married to a good man, had two precious daughters, a warm roof over our heads, friends, activities, possessions, and more. But I was empty. My soul was yearning for something that the things of this world could neither provide nor satisfy. A song that was popular at the time typified my life. It was Peggy Lee's "Is That All There Is?" The title said it all. I knew there was more. I just didn't know His name was Jesus. Through the loving efforts of two very determined women in my life, I discovered that, "if you confess with your mouth Jesus as Lord, and believe in your heart that God raised Him from the dead, you will be saved," and "For it is by grace you have been saved, through faith and not of yourselves… it is a gift of God" (Romans 10:9–10; Ephesians 2:8).

In 1982, at the age of 34, I gave my life to Christ, and He gave me His. It was a calm exchange—sweet. But difficulties lay ahead, and God knew it. As I look back, I am grateful for all He's done ... and sometimes I made it pretty difficult for the both of us (though nothing's too difficult for Him; I still marvel at both His patience and persistence). He used every pain and tear to mature me by His mercy, grace, and transforming power. And He will continue to do so until I join Him in glory (although I'd really like to hold out for the Rapture!).

 Judy

Suffering Alongside

In being honest, I am not writing from the mountain peaks. Instead, I sit before a screen with tears running down my cheeks. For the second time in too few years, I am sitting on my knees, looking out at the edge of eternity, wondering why God has handed my family a cup of suffering we aren't ready to hold ... again. I sit before you remembering the pain of grief and suffering, I once journeyed, wondering how it might be different this time. I remember how God was glorified through our story, knowing He will be this time as well.

In being honest, I sit in a space of contradiction. I cling to the hope of my Jesus. I have experienced His inexplainable peace. I have experienced the richness of His grace when the ground beneath my feet was crumbling. He met every need in ways my family and I could not have begun to imagine. I know firsthand what it means to be renewed by God's mercy each and every day. When the pain was too great to bear, my Jesus comforted me. He held me tight in His arms and He healed my heart. My heart is not without scars, but I know the joy of Jesus in the darkest of days, and the promise of eternity is the most precious gift we carry through this life.

Through the tears, I know all of this to be true, and yet, I still ask, "Why must we walk this road again? Why have you chosen us as a source for your glory again?" Of course, I want to see Jesus glorified. I want to see people come to know Him through my story, our story. But 14 years isn't long enough. I haven't forgotten the pain. I never stop missing my sister.

I was 28 when we released my sister into our Savior's arms. My sister was only 21 when cancer shortened her time with us on earth. The dreams we had for the future here were shattered, but the hope and excitement of eternity deepened. The gap between the now and the eternal is a little smaller. Heaven is a little sweeter, if that can be possible.

My sister's battle was only three months long, but they were some of the most precious months we have shared as a family. The troubles of the world outside fell away as we turned inward and upward toward our Savior. We celebrated the day we had before us. It was truly a gift of time. There were so many highs and lows, much like a roller-coaster ride, but I had a peace that could only come from God because of the sacrifice Jesus made on the cross for each of us. In the fire, I found strength to selflessly pray on my sister's behalf for eternal healing if quality of life was reduced to endless suffering. I wanted her here so badly, but suffering in a hospital bed is not what any of us want to endure endlessly.

Luke's account of Jesus' prayer in the Garden of Gethsemane is unique from Matthew's and Mark's. In Luke 22:42–44 it says:

> "Father, if you are willing, remove this cup from me; yet not my will, but Yours be done." An angel from heaven appeared to Him, strengthening Him. And being in agony, He was praying very fervently; and His sweat became like drops of blood, falling down upon the ground.

Jesus knew suffering, but like any of us He didn't want to suffer. Suffering is unpleasant. Jesus prayed so earnestly His sweat was like blood. But did you catch the middle verse? An angel from Heaven appeared and strengthened Him. God gave Jesus strength to endure the path before Him. In 1 Peter 1:6–7, Peter wrote, "In this you greatly rejoice, even though now for a little while, if necessary, you have been distressed by various trials, so that the proof of your faith, being more precious than gold which is perishable, even though tested by fire, may be found to result in praise and glory and honor at the revelation of Jesus Christ." If, in times of great suffering, we press into Jesus Christ, we will find strength and He will be revealed. I can speak from personal experience: people are drawn into the story of those who suffer with Christ by their side. They want to know how one can suffer and still smile. They want to know how one can suffer and still experience joy. They want to know how one can suffer and still believe that our God is good. Through faith, God's light shines through the clouds of darkness.

Our world shattered as we said our final goodbyes. My sister was already whole, dancing on the streets of gold with her gorgeous brown hair flowing in the light of the sun again. But in our hands, we held pain, suffering, and grief alongside the joy, hope, and promise of eternity. I couldn't look elsewhere. Jesus was my strength. Without Him, I don't know how I could have endured the days that followed. Without Jesus, I don't know how I could have stood on a stage and delivered her eulogy. Without Jesus, I don't know how I could have found the strength to smile when the days felt heavy. We are not made for this world, and I know that someday all of this pain and suffering will fade away. What is the value of pain and suffering here if there isn't something greater waiting for us on the other side? Someday we will be reunited with my sister, and it will be so, so sweet.

As I sit here and write my story, we have just learned that my mom is now battling cancer. We are four days shy of the date we celebrate my sister's homegoing. To say the pain is raw would be an understatement. I do not know where this journey will lead. I wish I could tell you that the journey forward is easier the second time around. It is not. It's scary and it hurts so much, but I will remain at the feet of Jesus, clinging to the hem of His robe because He is our healer, even if …

 Heather

Such Amazing Grace!

Growing up in a home where we dressed up for church every Sunday, I attended parochial school, where I was taught if you were good you went to heaven, and if you were bad, you went to hell. At night, I would lay in bed reciting prayers until I fell asleep. When my bus to school arrived early, I would sit in the back of the church next door and listen to the service.

I knew nothing about God's Grace. When I made choices during my freshman year of college that were far from holy, I hid from God. Church was no longer a place I visited and my prayer life evaporated. It wasn't until I was teaching snowboarding my senior year at Penn State that I accepted an invitation to church from a co-worker. The service was different from anything I grew up with, and the lyrics,

"Better is One Day in Your House Than Thousands Elsewhere" resounded in my mind.

During my final semester, while studying abroad in Europe, I felt compelled to walk into the Cathedrals. One day in Rome, I entered a confessional booth to share the sin that had plagued me. To my amazement, nobody had been on the other side of the booth to listen. For the first time in my life, I understood a God who was so loving, that He would just want me to come to Him.

After graduating, I moved to Washington DC, just months before 9/11. I was working 2 jobs but happened to catch a story on television over my lunch break about a boy in a coma who experienced a miracle. A couple months later, I found myself in need of a miracle. I awoke to a phone call that my 50-year old father had a massive stroke. He had been found in the snow and now laid in a coma. Devastated and frightened, I found myself pleading with God to let him live. Days passed and doctors told my mother she would need to decide when to pull the plug, as he was not going to survive. That very next morning, my grandmother and I prayed desperately for his life as we walked down the long dark hallway to his room. As we stood there, my father opened his eyes for the first time since the stroke.

Having witnessed this miracle, I knew God existed. Still, the empty void I felt inside remained. I tried to fill it with things that were all so fleeting: people, vacations, cars, boats. I remember the evening I moved into my new home overlooking the marina and wondered why I still felt so empty inside.

While selling new homes, I came to be friends with an agent named Linda. We'd golf together and I remember my confusion when she told me she believed there would be murderers in heaven. She explained that Jesus died to take away our sins, so no matter what we've done, if we confess with our mouth that Jesus is Lord and believe in our hearts that God raised Him from the dead, we will be saved by grace. Our Creator loved us so much, He sent His only son that whoever believed in Him would not perish but have eternal life. And though our sins are like scarlet, He will make them white as snow, so that we can be in relationship with Him. For years, sitting in the back of a church, I had seen the image of Jesus hanging on a cross but I never considered that he died for me, to take away my sin.

Not long after, a Christian Radio station was playing in my car and a little girl shared a prayer, "Jesus, come into my heart and help me to know you more." I repeated the words and started to wonder, if you had Jesus in your life, what did that look like?

When Linda invited me to a group called Bible Study Fellowship, I reluctantly joined her. As I began to read my Bible, I was amazed at all of the beautiful promises God had given us. How had I missed knowing this all my life? This was remarkable.

Meanwhile, circumstances in my life were chaotic. My Mom was on a heart transplant list, my income was drastically decreasing as the real estate market was crashing, my expenses were now way over budget and my selfishness left my relationship on the rocks.

I clung to God's Word… "Look at the birds of the sky, that they do not sow, nor reap nor gather into barns, and yet your heavenly Father feeds them. Are you not worth much more than they?" – Matthew 6:26

Then, on my 31st birthday, I found myself completely alone on the floor of my home, crying out to God. The words of the Meredith

Andrew's song, You're Not Alone, that I had been learning to play on the piano, seemed to blanket me, as I realized I wasn't alone; God was with me. He became my Great & Mighty Comforter as I suddenly had eyes to see that He could make beauty from ashes.

That day, He took my stony stubborn heart and gave me a heart of flesh, with a love for His Word, that would sustain me, guide me and fill me with His fullness of Joy in His Presence; Such Amazing Grace!

 Michelle

God Does Not Disappoint

I grew up in rural upstate New York, in a small town, attending church in a tiny chapel. I knew many of the farmers and townspeople who attended our church, and as I approached my teen years, I realized that many of them lived and talked as if they knew God as a friend. I felt left out and I wanted that.

At age 15, while playing with kittens in the hayloft, I was asked by my cousin, if I died tonight, did I think I was going to Heaven? I said yes. She asked why. I said because I was a good girl. Susan told me what God said about that: "For by grace are you saved through faith, and that not of yourselves; it is God's gift—not from works, so that no one can boast" (Ephesians 2:8–9), which erased my reason for getting into Heaven! That year I read a book about finding peace with God, and the next summer I asked

Jesus to come into my heart and life and give me a new life—His life.

In college, I requested that God would give me a hunger and desire to read and study His Word. I've been doing that all my life. Purpose and fulfillment have come to me, guidance and peace, and deep abiding joy, even in hard times. God and His Son Jesus Christ do not disappoint. 1 John 5:11–13 has been a rock-solid promise for me: "And the testimony is this, that God has given us eternal life, and this life is in His Son. He who has the Son has the life; he who does not have the Son of God does not have life. These things I have written to you who believe in the name of the Son of God, so that *you may know* that you have eternal life."

 Jackie

All I Had to Do was Trust in God

My husband, Dave, and I were both raised in the church, and we attended every Sunday. That was the extent of our religious experience: one hour a week. We knew Jesus, but we didn't have a relationship with Him. Practicing our religion failed to satisfy us, and we began to realize something was missing.

In 2003, our son, Kevin, introduced us to his girlfriend's family, and that was our first insight into how a true Christian family lives. We were so impressed with their well-behaved children (all nine of them) and their loving, genuine ways that we wanted what they had. They never mentioned the words "Christian" or "Christianity" to us, but they didn't need to because God's love permeated every aspect of their lives and showed in their words and actions.

In the spring of 2006, Kevin invited us to attend a performance at the church where he and his now wife, Bonnie, attended. After the performance, Dave and I signed up for a class because it promised to teach us more about Jesus. After the class ended, our group continued to meet for a weekly Bible study, and I was anxious to learn as much as I could about Jesus. God placed a godly couple in our lives to teach and nurture us.

However, things were not going as smoothly at home as you might think. For years, I had been a social drinker, but in 2003, I started to drink very heavily. When I say drink heavily, I mean the pass-out type of drinking. Since Dave worked shift work at the fire department, I didn't have to account to anyone on the nights he worked. I still drank when he was home, but not as much. However, it must have been enough because he was concerned. Believe you me, I'm no party girl. I didn't drink in high school and only occasionally in college. I considered myself a nerd. So why the heavy drinking? I now realize it was an attempt to fill the empty hole in my heart.

As the drinking worsened over time, I knew I had a problem. It seemed every time I tried to cut back, I failed. In September 2005, Dave was deployed to Mississippi after Hurricane Katrina and was gone for 43 days—43 days of me not having to account to anyone. I remained sober on the nights of the conference calls to the families because, after all, I was the incident commander's wife and I needed to present a respectable front—a perfect mask. But, on the other nights, it was a free-for-all. One evening, I started walking over to my daughter's house because I wanted to play beer pong with her. Here I was, a 49-year-old woman, drunkenly walking up my street. Thank heavens God prompted me to go home before I was arrested for public intoxication. Another time, I ran out of liquor and actually took a swig of vanilla extract. It burned on the way down and I commenced coughing. I never tried that again. I was quickly slipping into an alcoholic state and couldn't stop drinking if I tried.

In the meantime, Dave and I were attending our weekly Bible study, and we hid my drinking problem from them. Months passed and I still had so many questions about God and Jesus; frankly, I was frustrated. I was waiting for that moment when God would drastically change my life and it hadn't happened. So the next time I had lunch with Kevin, I asked him, "How will I know when I'm a Christian?" He said, "I don't know, Mom, but let me pray for you." He prayed that God would remove any obstacle that was preventing me from turning my life over to Jesus. God knew there was an area in my life that needed to be changed, an obstacle to be removed, and He decided to address it the very next day!

It was a crisp, cool fall day and the sun was shining, so I decided to do some yard work. As I was raking the leaves and praying to God, I heard a commanding voice say, "Stop drinking." I abruptly stopped raking, looked up, and said, "What?" "Stop drinking." I wrestled with that voice for a good 20 minutes. For every reason I gave against stopping, the voice had a compelling argument as to why I should. For heaven's sake, I was going on a cruise the next month. Did God really expect me to go without drinking? Couldn't I just wait until after the cruise? The voice said "No." As my arguments weakened, I started to think about the sacrifice Jesus had made for me on the cross, and I decided that obeying Him would be the least I could do. As I contemplated that thought, I realized that if God wanted me to stop drinking, He would make it happen! Aha ... The moment of truth! All I had to do was trust in God.

I haven't had a drink since November 17, 2006. It wasn't easy at first. Satan had a stronghold on me, and he pummeled me with doubts. "You're really not going to have any more alcohol for the rest of your life?" "Really?" "What kind of fun will you have on your cruise when everyone else is drinking and you're not?" "Why can't you have just one drink? A lifetime is a long time to go without." Over and over, Satan taunted me. But I had learned that day to place my trust in God. Sometimes I still struggle with relinquishing control, but God is working on my heart. There's one thing I know for sure: After 50 years of relying on my own abilities, I put my trust in the One who saved me. I don't miss drinking now, because what I have in Christ Jesus is so much better.

❀ Mary Anne

The Still, Small Voice

I'm not sure how to start, so I'll start at the beginning. First of all, I come from here. I am a native. I grew up in Falls Church, and both of my parents worked for the government. We went to church every Sunday.

While I was in college, I was with a group of girls who attended a Pentecostal church. One night I "heard a still small voice" and committed my heart to Jesus. Jesus heard my cry of faith and has helped me in many ways ever since.

After college, I came home and eventually put together a Bible study group with some friends. It was there that I met Michael, my future husband.

Michael and I got married in January 1980 during the absolute worst snowstorm of the season. We moved to Alexandria and continued for a while with House Church. Sadly, my mother became ill and passed away. Then we moved to our present house in Springfield. I'd had a very interesting job (it was a paid job), reading newspapers from all over the nation, but then I got a job with the government. Due to various circumstances, House Church ceased to exist and Michael needed his Sunday morning rest, so I explored other churches. I went to a Bible church for a while and then ended up at a messianic church for a couple of years. There were a lot of ups and downs there, so I eventually came to Burke. Finally, Michael got caught up on his Sunday morning rest and began to attend with me.

 Eleanor

A Sunny, Warm Hug

Even before I became a follower of Christ, God made Himself known to me. I could feel God's presence in the soft breeze as we walked to church. I did not want to go inside because the sun wasn't finished giving me a hug.

We moved from the city to the country when I was in third grade. I still had the light breeze as I rode my bike. Even in a world that had spread out, God was still there. God helped our crops grow and gave us beautiful sunflowers that the neighbors would talk about for years.

Dad now drove a pickup truck. Sometimes Dad would drive fast on the dirt roads. My sisters and I were scared, and we would huddle in the bed, praying. We learned that God answers prayer because we arrived home safely each time.

We attended a church in our small town. When I was in fifth grade, my oldest sister walked down the church aisle when the benediction was being sung and asked the pastor to be baptized. Well, my middle sister and I were right behind her because we had been raised to stick together. I had no idea why we were going to get baptized, but my oldest sister always pointed us in the right direction, so I was in.

The pastor met with each of us individually. When he met with me, I did my best to answer his questions. He said he did not want to baptize anyone who did not know Christ. The pastor asked me to fill out this workbook to make sure I knew Christ.

As I filled out the workbook, I learned that my wrongs could keep me out of Heaven. God is holy and anyone who has made just one mistake is separated from Him. Jesus came and lived a perfect life. Jesus died on the cross and three days later arose from the grave. He did this to pay the price for my mistakes. I accepted Christ's payment for my sins and am thankful that there is no more separation from God.

A few months later, I would experience my first miracle at my baptism. Entering the water, I noticed the pastor's hands shaking. Strange! Then I was immersed in the water, as a testimony that I believed that Christ paid the price for my wrongdoings. Later, I found out the heater was never turned on in the baptismal and the pastor was shaking from the cold. But God never allowed me to feel the cold.

 Christine

The Love of God

"That's it?" I cried. "Yes," came the answer. I moved to the dining room table, but this time, little did I know, it wasn't to roll a joint or unpack some other drug. This time was a life-changer! I repeated a prayer that my friend led me in to ask Jesus to rescue me from this life that felt so out of control. When I picked up my head and opened my eyes, it was like seeing sunshine for the first time. I couldn't stop smiling. I seriously went from despair to joy in less than 60 seconds!

I was raised going to church, but my ears were closed to the love of God. When I was 13, I began hanging around with a motorcycle gang and smoking drugs. From there, my life spiraled downhill to a drug called blue meth. A few years later, I met a young boy who was a heroin addict and not very kind at all. Yet somehow, I was attracted to him. I was trying to break my relationship off with him but found myself pregnant. My plan was to raise this baby alone, but guilt set in, so when I was six months pregnant, we were married. This marriage I chose was off-and-on and pretty abusive. Over a few years, he had gone from heroin to methadone to alcohol and back to heroin. Always fighting and living in fear was wearing me down. Finally, after five years, I decided to secretly move out and found an apartment for me and my two small children.

This is where God had "set me up." The residents in the apartment building looked like this: several drug dealers, a same-gender couple, a pimp and his prostitutes, and my best friend with two children and her boyfriend. Then, on the same day I moved in, a pastor, his wife, and their two children moved across the hall from me. God was on the move!

During the first year in the apartment, the pastor and his wife became my good friends. As I listened to their stories of God's love, I just couldn't fathom it. Throughout my teen years, when I did something wrong, my mom would tell me that God was going to get me for doing that! Needless to say, I was skeptical and running away from God as fast as I could!

After a year of trying to clean up my life, I still felt fearful and full of despair. I ended up in the emergency ward, where the doctor thought I had a stroke or a heart attack. My white blood cell count was extremely low, due to a wrong prescription drug I had been given weeks earlier. Sickness, fear, and now despair had invaded my life with thoughts of dying and leaving two small children alone!

A few weeks later, my pastor friend came over to talk, and I just began crying. "You need Jesus, Debbie" were his soft words. After moving to my dining room table to pray, in 60 seconds or less, my life completely did a 180! My sins were forgiven. My body, soul, and spirit were revived.

Within these 40-some years of following God's way for my life, I married the man God had for me and am becoming the woman He created me to be—one that is no longer full of fear but full of hope. I'm constantly learning new things about the love God has for me, but that's another story of God's grace!

 Debbie

Finally Set Free

I grew up in the church and was very religious. I prayed and read my Bible daily. But at the age of 12, I became very fearful. I lacked any peace.

I attended a private school and was named "Most Christian Girl" in eighth grade; however, I thought that just meant being a good person.

In high school, I sought acceptance from boys and friends but still experienced times of fear. In my sophomore year of high school, I wanted to be a pom-pom girl. I was practicing with another girl, and we started talking. I asked her what church she went to, and she said she was a Christian. I had never heard of that as a church before, and I was curious. She told me that it meant that she had asked Jesus to forgive her sins and to be her Lord and Savior. I was intrigued but not convinced. My biggest concern was that I would have to give up all the fun I was having in high school. I talked with my mom about this, and she told me that the Holy Spirit would show me what to do.

The fears I had been experiencing increased, and no matter what I did to subdue them, they remained. One night, when I was afraid, I heard God in my heart telling me to just do it! So I went to my mom and crawled in bed with her. I told her what I wanted to do, and she helped me to pray and to ask Jesus to forgive me for my sins and come into my heart. I immediately had peace, but unfortunately it didn't last.

When I told my friends who were Christians about my decision, one of them said, "I thought you already were a Christian." I continued living the life I was living, and nothing changed ... including my fears.

I participated in a beauty pageant, thinking that if I won, all my problems would go away. I didn't win.

In college, I was involved in a Christian ministry, and that is where I learned how to live as a Christian. At one point, I had to decide to continue to follow Christ or to keep living my life as I knew it. It was like I had my feet in two places. Thankfully, I chose Christ.

Towards the end of college, I finally sought counseling to deal with my fears. My counselor was great, and I made a lot of progress ... but I still was afraid.

At the very end of my college career, I met my husband, Michael. God used Michael to teach me about His love and what that looks like ... but I still had fears.

After about five years of marriage, Michael and I attended a Sunday school class at our church. One morning while working on the study, all the head knowledge about God's love finally filled my heart and I knew He loved me. Finally, I was set free, literally, from fear. I would be lying if I said those fears never attempted to take hold of me again, but what I knew then and know now is that I am forever loved and saved by God, who will never, ever leave me nor forsake me.

One of my favorite Bible verses is Psalm 139:1 "O Lord, You search me and known me," because He knows everything about me and still loves me.

 Sarah

New Life in Him

I grew up in a loving, non-Christian home with all I could ask for materially. My mother could be very critical at times, and I was very sensitive. Putting her on a pedestal, I made it my life's aim to please her. Her approval seemed everything to me, and her disapproval crushed me, driving me to despair. I soon transferred this to other people.

One day when I was 12, I recall my mom reminding me to wash my hands after I used the bathroom, as there were germs everywhere. At a time when I considered her words gospel, I started washing my hands incessantly for fear of getting sick and dying. This was the beginning of my obsessive-compulsive disorder. It was totally fear-based. I picked up other OCD habits, like checking and rechecking, and having fearful thoughts of harming myself or others. I was terribly scared of what would happen if I didn't check or recheck, or if I acted on my fears of harming others.

In retrospect, I can honestly now thank God for my OCD, as it drove me into His all-sufficient arms at the age of 24.

At my wits' end because I feared acting on my obsessive thoughts, I cried out to Jesus after reading a book and watching an evangelist's revival. That was the beginning of my personal relationship with my blessed Savior and Lord. Although He did not deliver me instantly from this mental illness, He is sovereign and has used medicine, therapy, His other children who have suffered, and most importantly, His Word to heal me and give me new life in Him. To God be the glory!

 Page

Broken But Not Rejected

I am a broken person. Life has a tendency to do that—to break us.

In spite of my brokenness, God reached out to me and drew me into a relationship with Him. It has been said that Christianity is the only religion where God reaches down to us. In other belief systems, people believe that they have to reach up to their gods through their "good" works.

God, in His sovereignty and wisdom, initiated a relationship with me because I was spiritually broken. He then brought me to life spiritually and gave me faith in Him. I do not know the day or time when I became a fully loved and forgiven person by Jesus' grace, but He does.

My father's job led us all over the world. Having to make new friends every two to three years, living in strange new countries, and learning strange new languages was difficult for me as a child. I felt like an outsider looking in. That led to being a people pleaser in order to seek acceptance from others.

When I was 15, God gave me a deep desire to know Him better by reading the Bible. I was also excited to be old enough to be in our local church's youth group. Finally, a place where I would fit in and be accepted and loved by my fellow high schoolers. Unfortunately, this did not happen! I never did feel loved or accepted by them, but I think God used this to turn my attention to Him. I had a hunger for His Word, and I began reading it every day. God was becoming more and more real to me as I spent time reading His Word.

Later, as I prepared for college, I realized that I needed to spend time with other Christians in order to grow spiritually. I prayed that He would provide Christian friends when I went to college, and He answered this prayer above and beyond my expectations. I learned what it was like to live in community with other people who were passionate about loving God and each other.

God did not reject me because I was broken. Are you broken? Know that He delights in you. He loves you. He was willing to be broken for you.

 Kim

Telling the Old, Old Story

"I love to tell the old, old story of Jesus and His love." I grew up hearing hymns like this. I do not recall a time in my life when I did not know about God and His Son, Jesus Christ. Even as a nine-year-old, I knew that I had done wrong things and needed forgiveness. I accepted His offer of forgiveness the best that I knew how, was baptized, and my relationship with Jesus started to grow. I read through the entire Bible and had a hunger to know God.

When I started college, I took several Bible classes. But my professors, ordained ministers with doctoral degrees from prestigious universities, did not seem to believe the Bible. I became greatly conflicted as I heard them say things like, "This part of the Bible is merely a myth" and "Jesus did not really say that." I had no answer for their intellectual arguments. I had been taught, as a child of a military officer, to always honor authority placed over me—a teaching that had been unconditionally reinforced by churches I'd attended. But now the authority over me was saying that the Bible was not trustworthy. I struggled and felt betrayed by my upbringing.

The day came when I could no longer tolerate the cognitive dissonance. I escaped toward the far end of campus, headed for a nature trail that led to a river. I remember raging, feeling like I was standing in front of God, shaking my fist in His face. Frustrated and angry, I accused Him of lying. I told Him that I no longer believed in Him and would not serve Him.

I suddenly had an astonishing experience. I felt the love of God let me go. He was not angry with me; it was love that I felt. And He let me go. I have tried to explain the feeling, and the closest analogy I could make would be to say that I went instantaneously from the atmosphere of God's presence to a place that could only be called a dark vacuum an infinite distance away from Him. It was like something from a science fiction movie, but what I felt in my spirit was definitely not make-believe. I had turned my back to God, and I was completely, utterly empty.

Fear and uncertainty shuddered through me. "I think I've made a mistake ... " I do not recall even finishing the thought before the next amazing thing happened. It was as if I had just barely begun to turn back to look over my shoulder at the God Whom I had just rejected. But before I could turn all the way around, the vacuum and all of the infinite distance between me and God vanished. I was instantly back in His presence. He seemed to be leaning forward on His throne, His hand to His chin. I felt Him smiling as He asked, "Yes?" It was an invitation, a singular, life-changing moment that I will never forget.

I encountered the God of the universe on a nature trail on my college campus. As I walked that trail, I began to learn about the fear of the LORD. Since then, God has faithfully led me in the path of righteousness for His name's sake. This is my story—the old, old story of Jesus and the extraordinary love of the one, true, and living God. How I love to tell it!

 Whitney

Walking with God

I was raised in a loving, churchgoing family in Indiana. I attended church every Sunday from an infant through high school, including church camp and youth programs. My denomination quoted scriptures, but I do not remember reading or studying the Bible much, and most of the congregation did not bring their Bibles to church. I don't recall ever hearing about a personal relationship that I could have with Jesus as a decision on my part.

As I left for college and later in my job as a flight attendant and in marriage, I fell away from going to church or praying. I loved God but felt a distance from Him, and He was not part of my life. I pushed Him aside to disobey all that I knew and was not on the right path. I did many of the "right" things by being kind and thoughtful to others but knew deep down I was not where I should be with God.

In 1978, after returning from living in Germany for three years, my Air Force husband and I and our two small daughters were stationed in Phoenix. Just before coming back to America, our first born daughter was diagnosed with a brain injury from a surgery that occurred shortly after her birth. I was determined to make her "right" by performing an intense therapy program, which had to be done at home for five hours a day, 365 days a year, with no breaks. It was a stressful time, trying to also care for our other daughter, who was just 16 months younger.

A friend, who was a leader at a large women's Bible study, invited me to attend with her. She saw that I needed the strength I could get from my faith in Jesus and not just a reliance on myself. I was able to get a volunteer to continue the therapy while I joined her once a week. As I sat in the church, I kept hearing the message about what it meant to be a Christian. I felt confused. I thought I was already a Christian, as my parents had raised me in the church. The teacher of the class invited me and my husband to be guests at a very nice resort in Scottsdale as part of their dinner party ministry. A testimony was given by a fighter pilot, like my husband. I was very surprised that I made a personal decision that night to ask Jesus Christ into my heart and life. From that moment on, I felt I was a new person. I was anxious to grow and learn more about Him and rely on Jesus instead of myself.

As a follow-up to the dinner, my husband and I attended a couple's Bible study. Together we learned that God had a plan for both of us and our family. I knew that through my belief in Jesus, His death and resurrection, that I was forgiven all my past mistakes and bad decisions, as well as my present and future ones. He has given me a new way of life as I trust in Him moment by moment.

Life has not been perfect just because I am now a Christian. Troubles do not go away, but they are so much easier to handle with Jesus by my side. He has held my hand through having a second disabled child; through a horrific fire accident with my son; having my own surgery for a brain tumor; and other significant and less significant trials. God has been with me through it all. He has brought so many wonderful Christian friends into my life who have loved me and supported me over the years.

I often say I am "walking with God," which is another way of saying I am living a life of loving fellowship and harmony with Him with trust and faithfulness. Through my simple decision to trust God, I can "walk" with God, having new hope and power through the gift of Christ's Spirit in me.

I am now a teacher at WOW (BCC's Women of the Word ministry) and feel so fortunate to rely on Christ each moment of my life and look forward to knowing Him better each day.

A verse that is very dear to me is Philippians 4:6–7: "Be anxious for nothing, but in everything, by prayer and supplication with thanksgiving, let your requests be made known to God. And the peace of God, which surpasses all comprehension, will guard your hearts and your minds in Christ Jesus."

 Jane

No More "Futility of Life"

"Life's a b**ch and then you die."

This phrase, popular in the 80s, reflected the inner turmoil of my heart. I rehearsed this idiom in my mind and often aloud whenever my life circumstances were particularly stressful or distressing. I was a very fearful child, teen, and young adult. I was filled with anxiety, displayed OCD behaviors, and was constantly afraid.

I was raised in a denomination which didn't overtly stress a relationship with God available through faith and repentance in Jesus Christ. Many of my fears surrounded my faith. "What if I mess up?" "What if I'm not good enough?" "When will God be fed up with my sin?" "When will grace run out?" Clearly I had no understanding of the truth of the Gospel. Legalism (trying to measure up, obey God in my own strength) was all I knew.

One day, in my early 30s, I was scrolling through the TV channels and I "happened" upon a popular televangelist who "happened" to be preaching about fear (clearly the Holy Spirit led me there). He spoke about how there is no fear in Jesus, shared the good news that Jesus died for my sins, and invited the watching audience to pray to receive Christ. At this point in time, I'm fairly sure I didn't have a complete understanding of being sorry and turning away from my sins. However, looking back, I see this as a turning point in my journey with Christ.

After praying this prayer, I began to attend a nondenominational chapel at Fort Benning in Georgia, as well as joining a weekly women's Bible study. I fell in love with God's Word. It was in my first Bible study that I understood I was a sinner in need of a Savior who took my sins upon Himself and died on the cross for me. I received Jesus and I was forgiven. Grace was lavished on me. I was rescued by grace through faith, not by my own doing; it is the gift of God (Ephesians 2:8).

I no longer held the "futility of life" philosophy. I fully embraced my new identity as a child of God. I no longer felt that life was a b**ch. Is life often hard? Yes, but now I see even the difficult times to be full of hope. Do I still sin? Yes, but if I confess my sins, Jesus is just and faithful to forgive me my sins and cleanse me from all unrighteousness (1 John 1:9). Do I still have times of stress and anxiety? Yes, but scriptures tell me to not fear because God is with me, to not be dismayed for He is my God; God will strengthen me and help me and uphold me with His righteous right hand (Isaiah 41:10).

I have never looked back. Some days the road to Christlikeness seems long and far away. However, I am promised in Philippians 1:6 that God will bring to completion the good work that

He began in me. I know that God is with me always. Jesus is Immanuel, God with us, and I am forever grateful.

 Diane

Thriving With Him

As a child, I grew up in a Christian home, attended church, and was eventually saved. I was baptized in the second grade, late in the evening on a weekday night, because I was both painfully shy and couldn't wait until Sunday. At that time, I knew and feared the Lord.

My childhood Christian life was fairly robotic: church on Sunday, VBS in the summer, and prayer at meals and bedtime. Then, at some point, we stopped attending church, and I succumbed to all of my doubts about following a man that had been raised from the dead. I started doing things my own way, with no thought of God. I had almost no relationship with my Creator. In fact, I can't even remember if I prayed around the time that my father died at only 43 years old.

As an adult, I never felt content—always restless. I battled that restlessness with a climb up the corporate ladder—but with each rung continued to feel the same hunger. I figured I wasn't satisfied because I couldn't tangibly see the good in the work I was doing. The next thing I knew, I found myself at the FBI Academy in Quantico, training to be an FBI Special Agent. It was at the academy that one of my classmates invited me to church with him, and I was forced to face my doubt and rebellion. Through apologetics and the mercy of God, I came to the unshakable conclusion that the hole in my heart that I had tried to fill with worldly accomplishments could only be filled by Jesus. I wound up marrying that classmate, and we built our marriage with Christ as a foundation.

The process of reconciling to God has been a journey of tearing down my old worldview, learning who God is, and discovering what He says about who I am to be. I had to build a relationship with Him. I remember the first time my new husband asked me to pray for just the two of us in our own home—I felt frozen, vulnerable, and frustrated that he had put me on the spot.

When I became pregnant with my daughter Anna, I continually prayed over His will for her care after my maternity leave and the best path forward for her to know and love Him herself. I felt I was faced with one of the biggest crossroads of my life with her birth—go back to the fast-paced life of the FBI or give up my greatest accomplishment and stay home with my daughter. As I attempted to discern His plans for me, I explored daycares, pored over our budget, and interviewed nannies. At each solution I found to go back to work, something would come up and our plans for Anna's care would fall through. When she was 10 months old, I felt God's clear answer to my prayer was for me to submit to His will and stay home with Anna.

My wild ride with the FBI concluded in July 2020. On my last day at work, I wept tears of sorrow as I turned in my badge and gun. We left our home in Massachusetts the very next day, and I started a new chapter as a stay-at-home mom in Virginia. In my new way of life, I prioritized space every day for time in the Word and learned more and more about His character and what He has done for me. Praying became easier as I came to have a relationship with my God. As my love for my Lord and Savior grew, so did my desire to talk to Him, to be in His presence and invite Him into more and more aspects of my life.

My grief over leaving a career that I loved quickly melted away as my identity was now solidly in the Lord and not in my career. I am thriving the more that I walk with Him. I am so thankful to the Lord for loving me so much that He would rescue me from my path of despair. He put me in a career to deliver me and then removed me from it to draw me closer to Him. He knew just what I needed.

✿ Shawna

God is HOPE!

Looking back, God was calling me from a very early age, but I did not fully respond to His call until I was married and moved to the USA with my American husband. God was calling me to read His Word (1 Samuel 3:9) and follow him. Finally, I obeyed after a friend loaned me a Bible, since I didn't own one. My first US friend just happened to be a believer! As soon as I started reading, I knew God had my heart and I was reading truth. It was like a light bulb going on. I did not know anything about the steps to follow and what to say. There was no one asking. I just knew I had given my life to Christ and He claimed me as His. I later understood the need for repentance, turning to Jesus, and laying down my life as a living sacrifice for the Lord (Romans 12:1–2). God gave me a burning desire to keep reading His Word and grow in Him.

Time after time, He led me to people who guided and helped me in my walk. Weekly Bible studies in women's homes became my life's focus. As I listened and learned, I started to grow in my new life as a Jesus follower. Radio shows and books, along with studying God's Word through Bible studies, became "living water" and spiritual food as I grew in the love and grace of Christ. Studying God's Word in the framework of fellowship, accountability, and opening myself to the Spirit's teaching has been so influential as I've learned to walk the life worthy of my calling in Christ. I am so grateful for the discipleship of the faithful women of God who have walked alongside me throughout my life.

Our lives rarely follow the path we desire or even pray for. God's ways are not ours (Isaiah 55:8). After several years of moves and adventures, we were transferred to the

Northern Virginia area for my husband's Air Force career. Months into the move, I was diagnosed with a very rare appendiceal cancer. I had to put aside most of what I was involved in and focus on recovering from a 12-hour surgery and huge chemo transfusion. As I sought God through these dark days, I claimed His great peace and trusted His path for me. He drew me closer as I drew closer to Him. He became so very present and comforting—just as He promised. God gave me certain verses through the journey that became so meaningful and carried me through, along with all the prayers of my friends and family (Isaiah 43:1b–3a). I had almost two years of remission and then COVID hit as we were moving again, hopefully anticipated as our last move. Six weeks after our move back to the North Shore, doctors found a tumor in my rib close to the spine. It was growing fast and too close to the spine to wait, so I had surgery to remove three ribs.

The aftermath of pain was excruciating and wore on for months, throughout an entire year. As I learned to lean into God and hear the Holy Spirit talk to me through the dark days when life seemed intolerable, God's presence was comforting and real. God had never been closer, yet all my worldly dreams were shattered and gone forever. I was and still am disabled and living an adapted life, glorifying what God has given me while letting go of what can no longer be. The cancer has now metastasized and is probably incurable, but for God! God is HOPE! Each of our days is numbered by Him. I rest in that and His care of me. I am gratefully living in three-month "chunks" as we go from checkup to checkup. These are gifts of three months of "normal" life with no treatments as we wait until it is necessary to start chemo to, God willing, keep the growth at bay, one day at a time.

God is faithful. I will praise him because He is so worthy of all praise (John 1:12). My prayer is that each person I meet will see Jesus living in and through me. May everything I am and have gone through point others to Jesus and His life-giving salvation as they believe, acknowledging that Jesus died for all our sins, repenting of their sin, cleansed by the blood of Jesus, who was raised and now lives, giving salvation to all who believe and choose to follow him, as we all wait for His return. Come Jesus!

 Christina

Joyfully Following My Old Friend

"I'm not going in there." The soft light from the stained-glass windows beckoned me. "It's Christmas Eve," my friend pleaded.

Christ's call came to me at a Christian camp when I was 13. I had accepted Him as my Savior. My mother thought differently. When I came home from camp and told her what happened, her response was "You did that in third grade." I suppose I had, through a couple of church rituals I participated in at the tender age of eight. I just didn't realize the purpose of it all until my mom said that. The main thing I recall from that third-grade experience was the man who practically represented God to me, hovering over me and personally scolding me in front of my friends and their families with these words: "You are more sinful than you think!"

Despite those rituals, I still consider Christ's call to me at camp to be my starting point. From then on, I struggled to live up to that call. I would give up, then run back to Him many times. The last time I gave up, I told God, "I cannot live as I should." I knew that man was right; I was more sinful than I thought. In fact, I was too sinful to be a Christian.

"I'll wait here," I told my friend, and I remained in the comfort of the dark car while he went to church.

A few years later, I fell in love with a man who was to be my future husband. Early in our relationship, he invited me to his church. Because of my love for him, I went. Just as I suspected, I felt the presence of my old friend Jesus. I couldn't resist Him. I welcomed Him back once again, picked up my burden of guilt—way more heavy than the last time I carried it around—and stumbled forward into a life of good deeds in an attempt to even things out.

A few more years later and in His compassion for me, Jesus sent two women into my life who offered to study the Bible with me, since I had admitted to reading it but not understanding much. They pointed to Romans 3:23–25 and Romans 7:15–20. "Jesus," they explained, "has paid for all your sins. No one is sinless but Him. We will never be worthy of His love. It's not who we are; *it's Who He is*." I realized all these years I had mistaken the conviction of the Holy Spirit for judgment. Now the truth blazed brilliantly in my mind and Satan shrank back, along with his lies and accusations. I let go of the guilt and shame I had carried and claimed the promise of Christ to cleanse me of all sin: past, present, and future! With this new understanding, I was baptized as an adult.

Daily Bible reading and prayer became a pleasure. To remain faithful, I knew I needed to have other Christians in my life, so attendance at church was a must for me. Serving to please the Lord rather than to earn acceptance brought me a spiritual joy I'd never known before. I traded guilt for gratitude that the One who is faithful and true had never given up on me, and never would. I traded the struggle of my back-and-forth spirituality for humble acceptance of the need I will always have for my Savior. I pick up that cross daily and try to follow Him wherever He leads.

 Kathy

Christ Redeems Broken Things

I guess I should begin in the middle and work my way to the beginning and then end with the obligatory happily-ever-after.

My name is Tanya Cooper. I have a young adult daughter. It's just me and her, and it has been that way for more than 10 years now. Her father and I divorced when she was young. I'm content, he's happy, and she's broken—broken-hearted, broken spirited, broken down—like a wind-up toy that won't run anymore, she's just plain old broken.

I did that. I broke my daughter. At least, that's the way I thought of it at the time. But I'll get to that a little later.

My daughter didn't understand why two seemingly intelligent adults who called themselves loving parents—who, of course, love and adore her—couldn't get along well enough to stay together in the same house. Well, honestly, neither did I.

Now let's move to the beginning.

I asked Jesus to be in my life when I was 15 years old. That same year I prayed about my future. I prayed for a child (strangely and mistakenly not a husband). I prayed that when it was time for me to have a child, it would be a girl. Right then and there, I heard the Lord tell me yes. I was elated.

Though I had asked Christ to be in my life, I didn't quite know what it meant to commit and surrender my life to Him, the way He does things versus the way I think they should be done. I continued to live as I thought best, or more to the point, as my mother thought best, as had always been the case. I grew up in a single-parent household and Mother ruled. I do believe I was more afraid of her wrath than God's. I lived in her house, played by her rules, and usually did as I was told. My teen years were slightly rebellious, but nothing unusual: still her house, still her rules.

However, it was her steadfast, unshakeable, Christlike daily modeling that brought me, my stepfather, her mother, and five of her siblings to join her in living in the grace of Jesus Christ.

I was about 22 when the Lord decided it was time for me to move out on my own. I phrase it that way because I don't believe I made the decision to move wholly on my own. And I know for sure He picked the apartment I was to stay in because I didn't even have to complete the application before I was accepted. He had paved the way completely.

I was young, not just in age, but also in how I navigated my relationship with Jesus. I was His child, and I knew clearly the voice of my Father. When He spoke, I heard and understood

Him. My life was His. All my decisions about jobs, finances, friends—everything I put before Him, and He helped me work things out. Until ... well, let's just say if I had been Eve in the Garden of Eden and the "clever one" called Satan had come along and whispered things to me, I couldn't have claimed later that I had been tricked.

When I met my "clever one" and he began to whisper, I knew exactly what he was saying and exactly what he meant. But before I took what he had to offer, I did what I always did before I made a decision. I took it to my friend Jesus, but this time I knew better than to ask His advice or council. This time I closed my eyes, bowed my head, and told my friend, my Father, that I was going to go. I was going to take this giant leap into the unknown, do what I wanted to do the way I wanted to do it without asking. And because I knew there would be consequences to my rebellious actions, I told Him I would be willing to accept whatever would come, figuring I could handle anything He could dish out, or at the very least I was old enough to take it. Well, the last part turned out to be true. (What seems right in man's eyes turns out to be destruction.)

That was the decision that changed my whole life. Who knew that one day, one moment, one decision, and my daughter would be broken before she had even gotten here.

Well, being a true friend, Jesus let go of my hand, but He never left my side. He let me go my own way and do my own thing, but He was always there, still telling me which way I should go. Pointing the way out, the way I never took.

I took what had been offered me, and in a 10-year span I had become promiscuous, dropped out of college, bought and lost a home, lost my job, lost my church, alienated family and most of my friends, and I'm pretty sure lost my mind, but I never lost God and He surely never lost me.

When I woke up and realized I was the one destroying my life and I could make the decision to stop it, God was right there with His arms outstretched to help me. But by this time, I was married and my relationship was already spiraling out of control, and our child was caught dead center.

I loved my husband, my daughter, my family, and I didn't want to lose what thread of an existence we had. We were all fragile, teetering on the edge. I was scared. But now I knew what to do, who to call, who to turn to, and it wasn't to my own way of doing things … not anymore.

Again, I closed my eyes, bowed my head, and told my friend, my Father, that because of our selfishness my family and I were in trouble.

I asked for forgiveness and for a way forward, and then I did something I almost never do—I sat still and quiet, waiting for His instruction.

That was 11 years ago. I'm now divorced and worship in an amazing church with amazingly loving friends who not only care for me but pray for my family. My daughter is now a young adult with a Christ-redeeming story of her own, and the best part is that God changed our relationship with each other into something more like friendship than frenemies. We are definitely still a work in progress, but we're better now than we ever were.

The once-upon-a-time happy ending will be when we see Jesus face-to-face. Until then, I know Christ as the one who redeems broken things, broken people, and broken relationships. God is now using me and my (actually His) story to encourage others in whatever season of life they are in.

I know now more than ever that His love and His faithfulness endures forever.

✿ Tanya

The Line Between Birth and Death

Life would be nothing without words. Imagine grunting for someone's attention all day. Words are a medium of understanding on multiple levels. Take this one: *sonder*. The very definition of this word is an epiphany. It means "the realization that each random passerby is living a life as vivid and complex as your own." Chew on this word, taste its excellence, and live its truth. My name is Rachael. I invite you to step in my shoes, open up my umbrella, and walk in God's rain of favor and encouragement. I can see where God has blessed me over the years, and now He is returning me to my home church of Burke Community.

My testimony starts off the same as most. My family attended church nearly every Sunday and even most Wednesday nights. I don't really have a story of life before Christ, because He was always in it. I also don't really have an "altar call" moment. Something that helped me grow close to God and make Him a personal friend was just sitting back and learning to be in awe of Him. He provided opportunities for me to be in awe by showing me fascinating things in nature. For example, I learned about *laminin*. It's a microscopic protein found in animals and humans. It's also the shape of a cross! It was amazing to learn that the literal building blocks of creation were constructed with the holy symbol of Christ's suffering and God's promise of redemption. Knowing this made God more alive to me than just reading stories like Noah's ark. Discernment was the next thing. God sometimes gently prods at my spirit. God has told me when shows, music, and books were not right for me. I've been drawn closer to God by listening to His direction. Lastly, He has been gracious. Lots of times, His warnings would be proportional to the degree of sin. But there have been cases where He has been kinder to me than He could have been. Knowing this has made me more grateful for His mercy, so I try to change and do the right thing.

Some areas where God has transformed me have been with emotional and physical struggles. I have wrestled with fear almost my whole life. I had a fear of planes, weather, and, sometimes, even eating. God has helped me to put more faith and trust in Him. I got over my fear of flying, and two years ago I flew more than 10 times by myself to and from other states for college and work. After I lived in Kansas and Missouri, I have gotten over my fear of weather and just use storms as a time to pray and rely on the Lord's goodness and sovereignty. Last year, the Lord healed me of lactose intolerance, and I have been able to eat without fear of getting sick, losing weight, or missing out on life! Praise God!

When introducing themselves, most would start by rattling off about their accomplishments or their childhood. As I get older, I realize how little those things matter. Not everyone was an army brat and grew up moving every three years. Not everyone was bullied in school or pulled out to homeschool. Not everyone gets to live in Hawaii for a time. But what everyone does have is a heart that needs to be held and loved by the Father. The more time goes on, the more I am focusing on Him. If our life is the line between our birth and death dates, the one thing I would want people to take away from mine is that even though I may be unworthy, God collects my tears in a bottle and will love me anyway. One way we can experience His love is to look strangers in the eye with sonder. Behind their pupils is a soul that we can reach by being God's hands and feet. When we do that, we will feel God's heart pounding in our chest. Understanding sonder leads to love, and when we love, as He did, we will one day hear those coveted words, "Well done, good and faithful servant."

 Rae

A Praying Mother

My mother grew up in church, and she trusted Jesus as her Savior as a child. It would be years later as an adult that her relationship with Christ would become real and vibrant. She had married a very handsome Airman after a two-week whirlwind romance – a man who did not share her faith. So, she prayed....... for 11 years she prayed that her husband would give his heart to Jesus. God was faithful and answered her prayers. My mother persuaded my father to take our family to a meeting at a local high school where an evangelist was preaching. His message was not sugar coated. Without Jesus we would spend eternity separated from God in Hell – yes, a real place. The decision for this 9-year-old girl was simple – I wanted to be with Jesus! I heard that Jesus paid the price for my sin. I could never be good enough to earn this salvation – it is a gift bought and paid for by Jesus! As I walked to the front of the auditorium to respond to his invitation to give your life to Jesus, I felt a hand on my shoulder! Was God touching me???? I turned around to see my father walking right behind me! Together we prayed and gave our lives to Jesus that same night – August 9, 1963.

Our family started faithfully attending church. We read the Bible together at home. I grew in my faith through Sunday School classes, youth groups, service opportunities and my own personal Bible reading and prayer. My faith grew as I learned more about God.

I experienced challenges during my teens that really kept my mother on her knees in prayer! My father served in Vietnam for a year, leaving her as a single parent during those rebellious years. I am convinced that it was her faithful prayers for me and her utter reliance upon God that kept me from making mistakes teenagers make with long reaching consequences.

I had an amazing opportunity to sing in a Jesus Band in the 70's. We would set up our band equipment on the parking lot at local Roy Rogers restaurants in the northern Virginia area. We would sing 3 or 4 songs, take turns sharing our "testimony" and then the preacher would give an invitation to the crowd to give their lives to Christ. Several band members had such "exciting" stories – how God saved them from abusing drugs and alcohol. I loved hearing them share. I dreaded the times it was my turn to share – because my story was so "boring." One night after sharing my story, a woman approached me. She said, "Young lady, your story makes me realize that even I need Jesus!"

Do good people need Jesus? The Bible says that there is no one good enough to meet God's standard of holiness! We miss the mark (sin). Jesus gave Himself as a sacrifice – the Only one without sin – to pay the price that God requires.

What about you? What are you depending on to gain eternal life with God? When my life on this earth ends, I will spend eternity with Jesus – not because of anything good I have done – He did all that for me! He did that for you! That is Good News!

 Pam

EPILOGUE

Dear Reader,

Have you ever wondered if what the Bible tells us is true? What if we knew for certain that Jesus is God, that He humbled Himself and took the form of a baby born to a Jewish couple two thousand years ago, for the purpose of taking God's just judgment against sinful humanity upon Himself? What if He really was resurrected afterwards and His promise is true that believers will also be resurrected? What if we allowed ourselves to believe that all our personal wrong-doing in our past, present, and future lives was forgiven and God stood with open and loving arms, beckoning us to trust in His loving act of dying on the cross as the God-man Jesus, what would life really be like?

Contrary to what some might say, true Christianity is not about what we do, it is about what He did on the cross. True Christianity is not a series of tasks to complete but consists of a simple relationship with Christ, the living God.

"For by grace you have been saved through faith; and that not of yourselves, it is the gift of God; not as a result of works, so that no one may boast." Ephesians 2:8-9

In the preceding testimonies, you stepped into the lives of several women as they took that first simple step into a relationship with Jesus Christ, trusting in the death and resurrection of Jesus Christ to serve as God's forgiveness for their sins. You saw how their lives were changed just by a single prayer of belief to Christ.

"If you confess with your mouth Jesus as Lord, and believe in your heart that God raised Him from the dead, you will be saved; for with the heart a person believes, resulting in

righteousness, and with the mouth he confesses, resulting in salvation."

Romans 10:9-10

If you find yourself hoping all of this is true, know that no matter where you are in your life right now, you too can have a relationship with Christ. There is no sin too great that His death did not cover it, and no one is ever too hopeless that Jesus cannot save her. In fact, if you are reading this book right now, you can be sure that He sees you and is calling you. He knows all about you, and still He loves you as His very own.

"You will seek Me and find Me when you search for Me with all your heart." *Jeremiah 29:13*

If this is true for you, you need only pray a simple prayer like the one below to start your own journey with Christ as Lord of your life.

The Believer's Prayer

Heavenly Father, I come into Your holy presence recognizing that I am lost in my sin. I am in need of a Savior. I accept the sacrifice of Your Son, Jesus Christ, who laid down His life for me. This day I choose to believe in Him and be completely forgiven. I allow Jesus to reign as Lord of my life forever. I follow His narrow road and enter the Gate to eternal life which is Jesus Himself. Thank You for drawing me to Your kingdom. Thank You that I am now and forever Your child. Amen.

If you would like to discuss how to know Christ as your Savior, please contact us at 703.250.3960 or email

Women@BurkeCommunity.com

We would love to hear your story, email us at

Women@BurkeCommunity.com

For more information about the community of Burke Community Church, visit our website at BurkeCommunity.com

Made in the USA
Middletown, DE
28 November 2023

43836459R00066